1/LT. M.L. McCloud
4520 Squire CIR.
Bouldu, Colo.

GRASS ROOTS APPROACH TO INDUSTRIAL PEACE

GRASS-ROOTS APPROACH TO INDUSTRIAL PEACE

Planning and Promoting Area Development
Through the Labor-Management Community Council

by

LAWRENCE L. STEINMETZ

BUREAU OF INDUSTRIAL RELATIONS
Graduate School of Business Administration
The University of Michigan
Ann Arbor, Michigan

Table of Contents

Foreword

Whether Jackson, Michigan, deserved the poor image it had ten years ago in labor-management relations can always be disputed, but it is a fact the image was there even though the actual strike history of the community was not nearly as black as that of many other communities.

Such an image was not helpful in carrying out our organization's purpose: namely, to persuade local industry to expand locally and to attract new industry into the area.

Recognizing one must have an attractive community to attract investment capital, we established the Jackson Labor Management Conference Board to determine if real or imaginary problems existed in the labor-management field.

After the suspicions of each group toward such an idea wore off and individual participants concluded the labor-management conference board was formed truly to benefit the community, problems were openly expressed and suggestions actually made by labor representatives as to how management might solve some of these problems .... and vice versa.

Today both labor and management representatives have kind words for the Board varying in degree from moderate praise to glowing terms. I do believe the functioning of such a board has had a favorable effect on managements' decisions to expand at home and has helped to allay employees' fears of his employer running away to alleged greener pastures.

The very existence of such a board has helped make our community attractive to our own companies as well as those viewing us from the outside.

Professor Lawrence Steinmetz has produced a thoughtful and thought-provoking survey of the labor-management conference board idea. Anyone interested in labor management relations, whether one of those people who live with this subject every day, or community leaders who would like to see improvement in this field, will discover this fast-paced writing of Larry Steinmetz stimulating as well as informative.

John F. O'Neill
Executive Director

Acknowledgement

This report is designed to present an analysis of labor management conference boards, their formulation and operation. Though the findings should be most useful to men who are vitally interested in the welfare of their community both from the standpoint of economic growth and development and labor harmony, much information will be of special interest to city planners, managers and council members.

Though the author bears the sole responsibility for the material presented in this report, valuable suggestions were made by many individuals. Professor George S. Odiorne offered constructive suggestions and comments; Albert W. Schrader, William H. Price, and Gerry Storch all suggested style changes designed to enhance the readability and clarity of presentation of material, not to mention other editorial advice and comments; Ruth McClellan, Mary Bessee, Sue Hudson and Kathleen Ceriotti all attacked various stages of the typing, retyping and proofreading the manuscript.

Further, a special note cf thanks also goes to Mr. John F. O'Neill of the Jackson Area Industrial Development Corporation for his continued advice and assistance in preparing the manuscript, as well as Carl Saunders who also served as a reader and source of encouragement and Lola Thyne who assisted in the compiling of some of the factual data included in the study.

To these individuals, and to the businessmen and union leaders who cooperated with the author during the study (but who, because of the nature of the information discussed, must remain anonymous) and to my wife Sally, who served not only as an editorial advisor, but also as typist and confidante, I offer my sincere thanks and hopes that their combined efforts will make this a meaningful publication to communities experiencing present and/or potential economic straits caused by labor-management disharmony.

L. L. S.

Boulder, Colorado
September, 1966

I

Conference Boards:
Need and Rationale

Situation: You are a businessman in the city of Midweston. You're also a member of Midweston's Area Industrial Development Commission and have just finished reading a private consulting agency's evaluation of the city's labor climate and prospects for attracting new industry. Some of the findings of the report are worrisome:

"The level of wages paid by Midweston industry is among the highest in the region, but there is an absence of correspondingly high levels of labor productivity."

"Wage levels in the area have prompted some Midweston concerns to expand elsewhere. They have also prevented other companies from moving in, although most people consider Midweston 'a nice place in which to live.' "

"There is some indication of a disinterested attitude on the part of city government and the population at large towards strikes in the community. Management has a neanderthal outlook on personnel relations, while labor unions are shortsighted in their contract demands. Each side has a chip on its shoulder, daring each other to push it off."

"It is possible for Midweston to take steps to remedy many, if not all, of these problems. But unless the community as a whole is willing to recognize its weaknesses and act on them, the mechanics of the remedy will be difficult to establish and implement."

Problem: What are you going to do?

Jackson, Michigan was mired in these same circumstances eight years ago — a strike-torn, economically-depressed town with little hope for tangible improvement. Today, it is prosperous and its people reasonably confident of its economic future.

Much of the credit for the city's rejuvenation has been given to the Jackson Labor-Management Relations Conference Board — the first one of its kind in the United States.

This board has no formal power; it is no threat to the traditional rights of labor and management. What it does do is bring both sides together to talk issues out rather than fight them out. A basis of communication having been laid down, labor and management can then work together to promote the industrial welfare and development of their city.

The importance of communication, of course, is acknowledged by everyone interested in labor-management problems. Most companies attempt to provide a continuing, formal system of communications through such procedures as grievance channels and suggestion boxes. Unions have "crab" sessions and an outlet with their own newspaper.

But when these devices break down, no channel short of specific arbitration exists in small firms and most large industries to reconcile a problem peacefully. Relations between management and labor may linger in expedient indifference, or degenerate further into acrimony and open conflict. While it is possible, perhaps, for some strikes to come about when both sides understand each other perfectly well, many others happen precisely because communication is not as good as it could be. There are many strikes that should never have happened.

Such a breakdown is obviously harmful to both sides. Unfortunately, the damage is not confined to the disputants but spreads to blight the entire community. For example, retail and service industries are affected by the strikers' diminished spending, while material suppliers lose sales and cut back production. This forces further layoffs and cutbacks as the strike continues in its cumulative constriction of the local economy.

In addition to avoiding the personal hardships of a strike,

the community has another economic interest in promoting labor-management harmony through communication. A city with an unhealthy labor reputation will hardly be attractive to firms that were thinking of locating there. Nor will it be much of an encouragement for existing industry to remain home and expand locally.

Yet many small and medium-sized American communities tolerate one or both of these dreary conditions. They rationalize their lethargical attitude with a variety of commonly-heard excuses:

- Labor and management are so firmly committed to their present position that they can't be educated otherwise. Management thinks unions to be thick-skulled; unions consider management hard-nosed and out of date. Nothing can be done to change them, so why try?
- Things aren't as bad as they seem. Industrial animosity is a common trend throughout the country; strikes and bad feeling are the inevitable and necessary aftermath of normal collective bargaining.
- Bringing in outside help on a problem confined to two parties may only aggrevate an already volatile subject. Asking for bargaining without conflict is like wanting a winning team without hours of hard practice.
- Local actions are determined by bosses (international union or corporation headquarters) far removed from the city. Local people are just the helpless last link in a chain; they really don't control the situation.

Obviously, none of these "explanations" helps solve the community's problem. They are very convenient excuses for inaction, not blueprints for taking action. These excuses are no longer justified, if ever they were. The Jackson Board demonstrates that a city *can* lift itself up by its bootstraps if it truly wants to. It need not be expensive to do so, either; Jackson's Board has operated on only $40 *a month*.

The Jackson model, furthermore, can be applied to any American city, though it best fits communities in the range of 5,000 to 500,000 population. Indeed, it has been adopted with excellent results in at least two other Michigan towns — Sturgis and Adrian.

All three had a less than desirable industrial climate which prompted their experiment. Any community burdened with a similarly blemished labor reputation, or the potential and threatened exodus of companies, would certainly do well to look into the benefits provided by a Jackson board.

It would be unwise, however, for a city to wait until it gets into trouble before examining the idea as a hasty cure. A conference board cannot guarantee blissful marriage between labor and management, but it can put communication between the two on a regular, continuing, community-wide basis. It provides a mechanism through which interested people can do whatever is possible to foster the growth and prosperity of their area in an atmosphere of peace and cooperation.

This book will describe how the Jackson board was formed, how it works, what it has done, and what more it could do.

II

The Jackson Story

THE BOARD FORMS

Jackson is a typical midwestern manufacturing town of 50,000 population. It lies 70 miles west of Detroit and is heavily dependent upon the automotive industry. 1958 was a notably poor automobile year, and, as might be expected, Jackson was sneezing from Detroit's cold. Only 4.2 million cars were built, a disastrous decline of two million from the year before. The entire country was in a recession.

But Jackson, though vulnerable as a large supplier of auto parts, was suffering much more than straight interpolations would have suggested. While total national output fell 5.5 per cent between the third quarter of 1957 and the first quarter of 1958, Jackson's industrial production during the same period fell 13 per cent. Its unemployment rate at the beginning of 1958 stood at 10.5 per cent and by April had risen to 14.5 per cent.

During this time of economic crisis, when the apprehension of the Jackson citizenry was at its highest, the brutal report of an independent consulting firm galvanized the community into an awareness of its plight. The Fantus Factory Locating Service (now called the Fantus Company) of Chicago had been commissioned by the Jackson Area Industrial Development Corporation in 1957 to study the area's industrial climate and suggest means of attracting new companies. The report issued in February 1958, drew these unflattering conclusions:

- The level of wages paid by Jackson industry is among the highest in the Midwest. While there is some indication of specific industry groups in the city enjoying labor costs more in line with comparable

cities, for the main bulk of employers wage costs
are a serious competitive problem. This is coupled,
in many instances, with the absence of correspondingly high levels of productivity.

- This combination is particularly prejudicial to the
  smaller companies in the city, particularly those in
  the non-automotive fields. Fortunately, there is
  no shortage of labor, else the effect would be even
  more pronounced. An important nucleus of manufacturers, still in the great minority, is quite satisfied
  with the productivity of Jackson workers.
- Wage levels in the area have prompted some Jackson concerns, in need of more production, to expand
  elsewhere. They have also undoubtedly prevented
  other industries from moving into the city.
- The major problem facing Jackson is the decreasing
  ability of business firms in town to adjust to chang-
  ing economic conditions. Businessmen are more and
  more reluctant to introduce new products, new work
  methods, new production techniques, new training
  aids, and new personnel policies in their Jackson
  plants.
- A large share of the predicament can be traced to
  the caliber of Jackson management. Poor personnel
  and industrial relations policies are present every-
  where; a consistent philosophy is nowhere to be
  found. The views of Jackson leaders with respect to
  labor range from the neanderthal "We pay them
  handsomely for their work here, what else do they
  want? They still complain," to the paternal "We
  give them everything for a long and short-run security and still they complain."
- Union leadership (aided by an extreme shortage of
  skills and by the existence of relative full employment for 12 years after World War II) has used its
  influence without regard to the long-run profitability
  of firms. This has become so serious that union
  economics, grievances, bargaining, and publicity
  efforts have literally driven some Jackson firms into
  bankruptcy. Others have left the city or are con-
  sidering moving out. Still others have vowed never
  to bring new products or new production methods
  into a Jackson plant. The remainder are holding on,

trying to do their best in a situation where making a profit becomes harder and harder.

- There is some indication of a disinterested attitude on the part of the city government and the population at large towards strikes in the community... Unions and management each operate with a chip on their shoulder, virtually daring the other to push it off.

The Fantus report, harsh but embarassingly to the point, was, in retrospect, "the best thing that ever happened to this community," one resident now says. Among other recommendations, it suggested the formation of a labor-management conference board as a step to rehabilitation. The report urged a kind of "full-scale diplomatic conference on the local level" in which labor and management would state their long-run goals, explore the areas where they conflict, and then attempt to resolve the conflict.

Thus, the issues would crystallize into the nature of the effect of total payroll cost on the long-range growth of a firm, and what happens to it when the cost is too high. "This forum would," the report concluded, "in a sense be a self-educating device for unions and management to demonstrate that profits are not evil, but represent the device by which each of us are assured of our jobs."

The Area Industrial Development Corporation, which had sponsored the Fantus survey, accepted the proposal and has subsidized the board ever since. But because many of the details of the board composition and orientation were only vaguely defined, four men—a union official, a company executive, a clergyman and a representative of a public agency—in the end laid the groundwork for this unique board through their own personal efforts.

They contacted businessmen, union leaders and city officials to persuade each interest to consent to a trial formation. Unfortunately, the organizing drive involved more problems than merely finding an agreeable time to meet. It aggravated old wounds, telescoped existing distrust and created new doubts, all intermixed with the hope for something better. Some of the obstacles were overcome, some were side-stepped, others worked themselves out through time. In order to give an insight into the subjective delicacies that were involved in forming the Jackson board, some of the responses at that time of the men who were approached and agreed to serve on the board are now presented.

UNION REACTIONS

Labor participants unanimously agreed that to talk problems out would be a step in the right direction. Beyond that, their reactions differed.

Desire for participation. One union president said a board would help management realize the advantages of informing employees of the company's future plans. He felt that the introduction of new methods and new jobs would be better accepted by the workers if they knew about them beforehand.

A chance to listen. Another union leader said managers had a right to know what labor wanted; at the same time, the board would allow management to present its view to labor on mutual problems such as moonlighting.

Desire for sound management. One labor member thought that many businessmen had abdicated their authority to do what had to be done to help their firms. Board discussions could make management realize that responsible union members were not trying to steal away its rights; on the contrary, labor much preferred firm direction to indecisive leadership.

Distrust of management. In a more negative sense, a labor participant said he joined as a watch dog. He feared that the board might develop into a one-sided discussion by managers who would then attempt to dictate to unions.

Fear of losing bargaining position. Two members' initial reaction was that the board might be a way for management to trick labor representatives into becoming very candid in conferences and thus gain an advantage at bargaining time. They saw no point in what, in effect, would be pre-contract negotiations.

Fear of management default. Another union man feared

that management would now either expect the unions to answer all the problems of low profit and low productivity for it or relinquish all their privileges in lieu of being allowed to sit on the board.

Fear of membership distrust. Other union presidents were wary of what their members would think. If the purpose of the board wasn't clear to them, they might gain an impression that their local presidents were selling them out to management.

Exposure to public pressure. Some members thought the board would attract public attention and thus be forced to be too cautious in discussion. Further, they felt that anything they said at board meetings might be recorded and publicized out of context, thus giving unions an unfavorable image.

Union qualifications. Another member simply questioned whether the union presidents about to serve on the board were qualified.

MANAGEMENT REACTIONS

On the whole, management members expressed less suspicion of the other side, but did feel labor might gain disproportionately more from the board.

Means of communication. Most of the company members thought much could be gained simply by having a formal opportunity to inform unions of management feelings on certain issues.

Chance for help. By the same token, managers said they wanted insights on the feelings of labor so they could make sounder-based decisions. By this, they meant advice, not dictated solutions.

Publicity-shyness. Similar to some union members, most of the business representatives feared they would be misinterpreted on the board and suffer a backlash from the public.

Fear of losing bargaining position. Management also feared that union members might not be open-minded on the board and would try to jockey for position for future bargaining. It also feared the board would assume arbitral powers and thus steal part of management's rights.

Lack of precedent. Another common misgiving was that of not knowing what to expect. The company men had no basis to judge how the board would work.

HOW THE BOARD WORKS

The Jackson board is composed of 15 men: seven management representatives with a minimum rank of president of a company; seven from labor with a minimum rank of local president; and one moderator from outside labor and management. The board includes *only* the manufacturing field; retailing, services and other business interests do not come under its scope. The 15 members meet once a month over dinner to discuss topics of vital concern to the local industrial community. These have included:

- Manpower in the 1960's.
- Lack of productivity when there is conflict between labor and management.
- Predicted progress in Jackson during the 1960's.
- Advantages and disadvantages of annexing an adjoining township.
- How should productivity be measured?
- Possible solutions for the impact of foreign imports on employment in the Jackson area and on domestic markets.
- Profit sharing systems.
- Why should Jackson industry expand in Jackson?
- Bad work habits and how to eliminate them.
- Is earlier retirement under Social Security desirable?
- What can labor and management do to improve the Jackson economy?
- Productivity of pre-retirement employees.

The board, therefore, provides a formal channel for maintaining labor-management communication in Jackson on a regular, continuing basis. It attempts to stop strikes before they get started.

The board operates under four ground rules made necessary by the reactions stated above. They were enacted as declarations of purpose in order to give original members an idea of the scope of the board. But since no provisions for amendment were made at the time, the ground rules since have hardened into an unwritten constitution.

1) *No powers.* This rule exists for appearance's sake, since the board obviously could not exercise any authority without permissive legislation from the city. But the first members did fear that there was a possibility of the board dictating to management and labor; it was certainly necessary to allay those fears for good.

2) *No collective bargaining or arbitration.* Many of the men originally approached thought such a board would enter into labor disputes, particularly into arbitration. None of the members felt they were qualified to serve in such a capacity, nor did they feel a communications board was the proper medium. In point of fact, there has been some indirect entry on the part of several individual members who have broached a specific dispute during board discussion and relayed comments and advice back to the parties involved. This is only a slight relaxation of the rule, however; the board officially declines to enter into disagreements directly and has never done so.

3) *No more than one representative* (either management or union) *from the same entity sitting on the board.* This was established for several reasons: one member is enough to inform his colleagues of board proceedings; having two men from the same firm might interject bargaining into the board; and double representation might also dampen the candidness of discussions involving the management and union men from the same company.

4) *No publicity.* This rule puts to rest the union fears of being misquoted in a house organ and managers' fears of being misquoted in a labor newspaper. Therefore, no minutes are kept and, with one exception, no official statement has ever been issued by the board. It does not even have formal bylaws or statement of purpose.

ACCOMPLISHMENTS OF THE BOARD

Communication. All members are quick to point out that

their greatest reward in participating has been communication with labor or management. This benefit has not been limited to the board: other Jackson employers began to seek better labor relations through more effective communication.

More cordial bargaining. Typical is the comment of one businessman: "I used to think the union reps were self-centered blockheads whom you couldn't tell the time of day. But I thought I'd give this 'communications' a try. I had a problem, so I just told them what I thought. They said, 'You're right, maybe we can help you with that.' I didn't believe it until I saw the actual results. Now I just plain lay it on the line, and things couldn't be better. Of course, we frequently don't agree on some things, but we never used to agree on anything."

Mutual trust and cooperation. Carl Saunders, retired editor of the Jackson *Citizen Patriot* and former board moderator, believes the improved atmosphere has filtered through the board down to the entire industrial community. "The biggest accomplishment of the Jackson board is the atmosphere of understanding in the community, specifically the increased trust, confidence and cooperation between labor and management," he said. "Unions in general have discovered that management is no longer the robber barons of old, and, at the same time, managers have discovered that the typical unionist is not a window-busting, bomb-throwing radical."

Specific help. Concrete improvements as well as good will have followed from better communication. In one instance, a company president had indicated that a particular job could no longer be handled in the Jackson plant because its piece rate was too high. This, of course, fore-shadowed a loss of several jobs. The union unilaterally offered to make a time study which later reduced the piece rate, saved the jobs, and added to profits. The union had not questioned the sincerity of the executive's claim because he had gained a reputation for straightforwardness at board meetings.

Improved labor attitude. Better relations on the board, according to two company presidents, gave union leaders and members a more realistic grasp of management's problems and points of view. This has resulted in fewer unreasonable wage demands and unwarranted complaints, for a union now no longer feels obligated to fight trumped-up battles for the sake of beating down management.

New industry, more jobs. Since the board was formed eight years ago, there have been 31 more employers and 7,000 more jobs (an increase of 27 per cent.) Unemployment is down to 2-3 per cent. Indeed, the Jackson labor market has become so tight that in late 1965 the board found itself discussing means of filling certain job shortages. Local businessmen indicated that they could immediately hire 763 more workers; these included machinists, draftsmen, tool and die makers and other skilled laborers, but also desired were 167 "just plain good workers with good attitude and some aptitude."

Of perhaps even greater (although unmeasurable) significance is the volume of industry that now wants to stay in Jackson; there are numerous informal indications that many plants which would otherwise have departed have remained instead. John F. O'Neill, executive director of the sponsoring Jackson Area Industrial Development Corporation, affirms that the board is one of the strong points he cites in describing the city to prospective new employers.

Local manufacturing employment is up 7 per cent over 1958, whereas similar figures for non-manufacturing and government employment show only a 2.5 per cent rise. Thus, there has been a much greater increase in manufacturing employment since formation of the board, whose members are exclusively in manufacturing. And this trend in Jackson comes during a corresponding period of relative *decline* in national manufacturing employment.

Fewer strikes. There has been a 28 per cent decrease in strikes. This is particularly noteworthy in and of itself, but also because the board was not designed to be a mediatory or arbitral body.

Wider acceptance. When the board was in its formative stages, many of the men asked to participate refused to do so, seeing the new venture as unworkable and over-idealistic. But, through time, the board has become accepted, and some of the one-time skeptics recently have sought membership or permission to attend meetings.

Satellite. The Jackson board has served as a model for other industries besides manufacturing. In 1961, executives of construction firms and officials of building trades unions formed the Construction Industry Labor-Management Conference Board. It was set up to attack a few specific problems and not to be permanent, but before dissolving it campaigned for legislation against fly-by-night operators and began a pattern of communication at the policy level.

National recognition. Two other cities (Adrian and Sturgis) have adapted the Jackson board, and several inquiries about its purpose and operations come in each month. These are answered by the Industrial Development Corporation, since the board has no staff. Board members also are invited occasionally to speak at business meetings in the area.

WHY THE PRESENT MEMBERS SUPPORT THE JACKSON PLAN

All members of the board — both union and management — said their major reason for serving is a desire to further the public interest. During interviews, they mentioned a sense of duty to do whatever possible to maintain peaceful labor-management relations. Underlying this were more specific interests for each side.

Several union representatives said they strive to get a better grasp of management's feelings on upcoming bargaining issues, discussing them in an informal atmosphere rather than exclusively at the table. They felt their hopes have proved to be well-founded and that in at least one case a serious economic issue was not allowed to get out of hand. Another labor member spoke of the importance of public relations:

  • "Unions owe their existence largely to public opinion
    and therefore have an interest in what the public
    thinks of them," he said. "If they are to stay in
    business, the public must at least passively accept

them. One of the best ways to obtain acceptance is
for unions not only to cast an image of being for the
good of the community, but also to act accord-
ingly. Through activity on the board, a union can
not only cast an image of having the good of the
community at heart, but also reinforce its stand and
position in the community."

Union leaders also view the board as a potential scapegoat
for a promise they cannot deliver to their membership. If a pay
increase seems a lost cause, a local president can escape cen-
sure by saying the conference board had discussed the matter
and concluded that a salary hike at the present time would be
unwise for everyone concerned. Finally, the labor participants
continue serving on the board because they feel they are now
understood by executives. One said: "I have discovered that
management is not trying to knife the unions, and I feel that
they now realize that we, too, have our problems and don't just
have our hands out for more, more, more."

Management also knows it is subject to public opinion, to
the point of accountants including "good will" among the
assets of a company. Participation on the board helps a firm
become known as "public spirited," a reputation which certainly will not hurt its sales. Thus, it is possible for a company
to receive a direct reward for a seemingly intangible service.
Another direct benefit the business members report is their
opportunity to gauge the general current of labor thinking.
Knowing this, the company can work better with its own
unions in achieving amicable contract talks.

The community as a whole also has a strong interest in
maintaining a conference board. The city must keep its industry at home and in good profit, while always seeking to
attract more industry. In Jackson, southern competition had
been frequently cited by company presidents as a reason for
possibly moving out. They did not begrudge the high wages
they had to pay, but did recognize the hard facts of competitive life. They felt something had to be done to hold the
line against higher wages until low southern wages became

more equitable. Through the board, the executives found labor leaders to be sympathetic to the problem instead of rigidly antagonistic. Together, they worked to expand their community's strengths rather than exploit its weaknesses.

The board is also useful to a city as means of attracting more industry. The North may have the stigma of being a high-cost area, but many corporation executives have been quoted as saying that they willingly pay high wages if the work force is competent and stable. A conference board can help insure both conditions. Talking problems out keeps labor relations on a steady, even keel. Such communication also may discover and eliminate worker grievances that are holding the level of productivity down from what it should be.

As one Jackson resident sums up: "What were we to lose from the board? We had a bad climate to begin with and if everything went wrong, we wouldn't have been any worse off. As it is, things have been better."

An executive echoed that sentiment: "I was skeptical at first, but I certainly have to give the board credit for the trust and mutual cooperation it has put into making this town come to life. Five years ago every businessman in town was saying the town was doomed because of the unions. Now they talk as if the whole place is pulling as a team. Maybe it's just mass self-delusion, but if that's what it is, I hope we keep right on kidding ourselves."

NO PANACEA

There is little doubt that the Jackson board has significantly helped the city. Several important statistics indicate so, and everyone familiar with the board has praised it.

Yet it would not be accurate to give the board sole credit for better times in Jackson. Certainly the nation's overall prosperity extends its effects to the local level. Jackson's heavy dependency upon Detroit, after all, works both ways. In 1958, during one of the most disastrous years in automotive history, they suffered together. Now it is boom time for automobile manufacturers and suppliers, and Jackson is riding the crest of Detroit's wave. The board has not proved to be a cure-all panacea for strikes, either. Their frequency has decreased sharply, but they still can and do happen.

Nor should the list of successes imply that the Jackson board is perfectly set up. It isn't.

The next chapter will consider other types of labor-management conference boards, and why Jackson's kind is the best. It will also examine the satellites Jackson's board has inspired and how they have improved upon the basic model.

III

Other Boards

TOLEDO

In contrast to Jackson's hands-off policy on unsettled labor disputes, the Toledo Labor-Management-Citizens Committee actively sets out to end strikes. Its organization plan states its purpose as "the peaceful settlement of labor and management disagreements to remove the impact of industrial strife on the welfare of the community and its citizens."

The board is the descendent of the Toledo Industrial Peace Board, the first community labor conference board to gain widespread recognition. It was established in the depression of the 1930's, when rapid resolution of labor disputes was most critical. Hence the emphasis on "fire fighting" in the later board, formed in 1946.

In 1944, Toledo had the doubtful honor of being fourth in the country in number of man-days lost due to strikes. By the time its new board began to operate, it had improved to 49th place and since then has had only four better years. Thus, the impact of the board may have been limited, especially since Toledo has not been noted as a fast-growing metropolitan area with a fast-expanding work force.

The Toledo board attempts to become aware of disputes which are developing and to solve them if an open break occurs. This procedure does not soothe conflict before it becomes aggravated; on the contrary, the board waits until conflicts arise before entering them. Dr. C. K. Searles, chairman of the educational committee of the board and former dean of the College of Business Administration at the University of Toledo, noted this shortcoming in 1955:

"I question sincerely that we are going to make steps for-

ward in bringing together labor and management and the
public if we only consider trying to mediate and counsel at
their disputes. I also question whether the board is ever going
to accomplish its real purpose if, after labor and management
have come to a position where they no longer find it possible
to effect a conciliation, the board may be called in to help
bring about mediation. I think we need to go very much
farther, that is to find out the things which affect labor and
management and the public in these various discussions. Find
out, if we can, even before these disputes arise, how to bring
about a larger degree of harmony."

Recognition of these weaknesses has been followed by several attempts at correction. Quarterly meetings of members are
scheduled, but they have an impromptu nature and generally
deal with mediation or arbitration matters. The board has also
held educational forums and programs, but some have de-
generated into simple information sessions; others are training
seminars co-sponsored with other institutions, such as the
University of Toledo.

One service of the board, however, does have some special
merit: "preventive mediation." This means helping parties to
a dispute work out their problem by diagnosing each case and
suggesting a remedy before a strike develops. The board en-
courages any company or union with bargaining trouble to
discuss the matter with any of its members. The board then
appoints a panel to study the situation and call on the advice of
expert technicians in time study, accounting, engineering, and
so forth.

This supplants the usual process of mediation in which problems are not brought to the board until right before a strike
deadline, when the pressures and urgency of settlement make
a long-range solution difficult. But "preventive mediation" is
preventive only in the sense that it brings forward in time disputes which are almost sure to arise. *Unlike in Jackson,* no
effort is made in Toledo to prevent the problem itself.

There is a *second basic difference.* The Jackson board, sponsored by the Industrial Development Corporation, is used as

an attraction to new and more industry. For the Toledo board, economic development has never been a relevant object of action. Toledo has a separate Area Development Corporation and an Industrial Development Council to take care of such matters.

PRESIDENTIAL ADVISORY COMMITTEE

The President's Advisory Committee on Labor-Management Policy, established by President Kennedy, is similar to the Jackson plan in its objectives and operation, but differs vastly in scope. It is composed of seven labor members, seven management members and seven public members, including the Secretaries of Labor and Commerce, prominent educators and labor arbitrators. It meets one or two days nearly every month to discuss current labor issues and problems. (The Jackson board does not have public members, except for its moderator, or all-day sessions.)

Kennedy instructed the advisory committee to make recommendations for policies to "promote free and responsible collective bargaining, industrial peace, sound wage and price policies, higher standards of living and increased productivity." The Kennedy-appointed committee did respond with several minor efforts. It published reports on automation, collective bargaining and world competition — three subjects of national significance which would have been of some benefit to the economy had they been heeded.

Regrettably, under President Johnson the committee has deteriorated further. The reports mentioned above came out in 1962; since then, only one more has been issued, and this was only a summary of seminars conducted at the University of Pennsylvania, the University of Chicago and the University of California at Los Angeles.

Suffering from size, importance and distance from the firing line, the presidential committee has failed to promote labor peace and harmony at the national level. It has not been effective on important issues within its scope, such as federal labor law, federal employees and unionization, or major steel and auto contracts. It has been notable by its silence in the August-September 1964 UAW-General Motors disputes, the infamous Transport Workers strike in New York in January 1966, and the International Association of Machinist-Airlines strike of July-August 1966, all of which could have used help.

Certainly former Secretary of Labor Arthur J. Goldberg's address to the Executive's Club of Chicago in early 1962 now strikes a hollow note:

"The establishment of the committee is a matter of major importance in American industrial life. When this 21-man committee was first set up many people were skeptical about its value and possible success. When one looks back at the history of other such committees, such concern is understandable. While the results of this committee have not been dramatic, I believe that the skepticism has abated. The fact that the committee has continued to meet is a success in itself, especially when one remembers that most prior committees broke up before they even got started."

Mr. Goldberg (now Justice) was able to cite one other benefit, aside from the fact that the committee was still meeting: "We are getting many welcome indirect dividends. Local committees are being established to bring labor and management together in continuing communication. This is a most welcome development."

WHY THE JACKSON PLAN IS BEST

The Toledo plan has had good results in thwarting labor disputes. But, in the typical community of 500,000 population and under, this is only part of the problem. The medium and small towns also need to attract new industry, keep existing companies at home, overcome worker sluggishness and prevent economy-strangling disputes long before they arise — not waiting until they look ominous enough to call in outsiders.

The Toledo plan is too narrow. It attacks the effects but not the problem. There is emphasis on cure without sufficient procedures for grass-roots prevention. Perhaps Toledo's board fits the needs of its community, as, indeed, any conference board should — but if the problem is a compound one of economic stagnation and poor labor relations, it will not suffice.

The potential of the presidential advisory committee, if any, rests at the national level. But it will never be particularly beneficial to the local community and its problems. It is necessarily aggregative in nature; with the exception of America's giant industries, it cannot consider the problem between an individual union and company. Any mechanism to do so would require a huge outlay for offices, employees and operations.

The resolution of a local strike is just as important to the local community as a national strike is to the nation. But certainly there are far too many cities of under 500,000 population for the committee to even consider focusing upon them.

A similar limitation would hold true for any proposed state-wide board, which has been offered as a solution to the unwieldiness of the presidential committee. A state-wide board might be very desirable — for state problems. An overly large bureaucracy would be needed to deal with local issues, and there might be a problem of politics hampering the operation.

The Jackson plan avoids the disadvantages of these types of boards and provides other strengths of its own. It is organized around local business and union leaders — men who have a decided interest in their own community. If it prospers, so do they; if they prosper, so does the community. The members are on the spot when problems threaten or materialize; they can get to the heart of the problem quickly because of personal acquaintanceship and closeness to the parties.

Cooperation between labor and management is successful in dealing with general problems of competition, profit margins, new industry, productivity and the like because they are not left to the solution of any one particular man or company or union. Wherever possible, other men, other unions and other companies work through the board to help out. They do so without the cumbersome machinery of a national board and without (usually) the intense time pressure of the Toledo-type board.

It is important to point out that a community faced with a

serious local labor problem must: 1) recognize that a problem exists and 2) recognize that it can be solved on the local level. The Jackson plan is adaptable to a community of any size, although 500,000 and under seems the most ideal. All that is needed is a group of civic-minded men willing to sacrifice their time to advance their community's interest — as was done in Sturgis and Adrian.

ADRIAN BOARD

In 1959, one year after the Jackson board got underway, the model was adopted in nearby Adrian. This town had not quite sunk to the economic depths Jackson had, but its unemployment had risen to 14 per cent. There had been no announcements of plant withdrawals or closings, but foreboding rumors had started to circulate.

City officials, surmising that Adrian was developing an unattractive labor relations climate, decided to act in advance of a desperate, last-minute stopgap move. Their board was formed not only as a remedy, but also as a normal feature of any industrial community.

After three years of operation the Adrian Board's accomplishments included:

- Communication between labor and management improved greatly. Both groups learned that it is possible to resolve problems which used to be fought out.
- It persuaded local industry to remain and expand operations. According to the Michigan Employment Security Office in Adrian, 89 new employers have located in the area since 1959, and unemployment has decreased to 1.8 per cent of the local labor force.
- During the three years of the board's existence, not a single strike occurred. In one instance, there was a real threat of a walkout — until the board offered mediatory assistance in an ex-officio capacity. The late John A. O'Brien, former manager of the Adrian Area Chamber of Commerce, said that the disputants then were persuaded to realize the outside

interests and effects of a strike and managed to reach
accord.
- Now, Adrian is wondering whether it will have
  enough people to supply its new and expanding
  industries. The Chamber of Commerce anticipates
  a required increase of 9,000-12,000 employees—this
  in a town of 22,000 and a metropolitan area of only
  85,000 in south eastern Michigan. Allan Graybiel
  of the Adrian Federal Savings and Loan Association
  recently commented:

"We no longer need the conference board. Labor and management are both more grown up now. Things are really good
today in Adrian. We keep the concept of the board in the
closet, ready for dusting off. But the board did its job, and that's
why it isn't actively in operation today. In fact, it was one of
the new industries which the board was instrumental in bringing to Adrian that suggested we no longer needed the board."

STURGIS BOARD

When its board was being organized in 1960, Sturgis, Michigan, was nearing economic chaos: an average of two companies
a year were moving out. Officials in this community of 10,000
in central Michigan close to the Indiana border were com-
pelled to act.

The board has been successful from the start. Indeed, it was
successful even before the start as some of its original members
were credited with being instrumental in settling a 17-week
strike at a local plant. Since then, there has been only one
strike in Sturgis, and that was at a non-participating, non-
member company.

A spokesman for the board, former Sturgis Mayor DeForrest
Strang, believes the board's most significant accomplishment
has been the opening up of communication. Prior to formation,
he said, many managers were seeking employees with "strong
backs and weak minds," while unions were demanding "more,
more, more." These attitudes have changed — several companies revised their personnel policies to reflect more realistic

manpower requirements and work crew sizes, while unions
have become more fair in their requests.

"Employers, unions and workers," Strang said, "now all
understand what profit is and how the prospect of profit is
essential to the continued growth and employment in the community, the same as they understand, recognize and appreciate
the role of the union. Labor and management are communicat-
ing and the community is profiting by it."

IMPROVEMENTS ON THE JACKSON MODEL IN SUMMARY

Since the Adrian and Sturgis boards were based on Jackson's, there is a great deal of similarity among them. However,
some of the later modifications have improved the basic model.

Turnover in membership. Neither Jackson nor Adrian have
provided for changes in membership (except that union members must retain their office to stay eligible for the board). This
situation simply "happened" in Jackson, but was planned that
way in Adrian. The founders there reasoned that the longer a
man served, the more valuable his contribution became as he
grew increasingly familiar with the members and continuing
or likely-to-arise issues.

Surely, however, a point of diminishing returns must set in.
In Jackson, for example, as early as 1962 members felt that
they had exhausted the contributions they could make to the
board and that new men and new viewpoints were needed.
Now, four years later, many of the same men are still serving.
Each of the members interviewed said that such unlimited
tenure was not desirable. This is important, for the attitudes of
the board members themselves ultimately determine whether
it will be successful.

In a situation such as this, it seems unfair to leave it up to
the individuals to resign. They may be reluctant to do so for
several reasons: simple resentment at being asked to step down,
a possible loss of community respect for no longer appearing
to be civic-minded, fear that their business or union will suffer

because it is no longer represented, or pressure from within the organization to continue serving.

In contrast to this sort of impasse, the Sturgis board has successfully made provisions for turnover. Each member is appointed for two years; the terms are staggered for better transition. When a member's term expires, there is a specific provision for his withdrawal, guaranteeing a graceful exit. He may be reappointed, however, if he desires and if his services are desired.

Publicity. While Jackson avoids and Adrian avoided publicity, the Sturgis board actively seeks it. Its members say they want labor and management inside and outside the town to know that an attempt is being made to solve industrial difficulties. Thus, meetings are publicized and bulletins posted in each local plant so that all employees are made aware of board activities.

(Excerpts from two of these bulletins appear in the appendix).

Sturgis' results indicate that a good board should seek and generate publicity. In attempting to lure industry, a community cannot rely solely upon word-of-mouth advertising; tangible evidence of the board's efforts will yield tangible results. A printed brochure or bulletin psychologically lends an official and permanent appearance to the labor-management harmony.

Entry into disputes. As has been mentioned, the concept of non-entry has been basic to the Jackson board, and has been followed technically, if not always in the spirit. The very nature of Jackson's and Adrian's boards makes them subject to requests for assistance; in both cases, they have responded as informal mediators.

Sturgis attacks the problem differently. In a procedure similar to that of the Toledo committee, the Sturgis board will formally lend its services to prevent a strike or end one if a party requests so in writing, and the steering committee of the board approves. The board has yet to act in this capacity, however, due to the lack of strikes. The procedure seems to be worthwhile. It makes Sturgis' board more ready and able than Jackson's to discuss specific disputes, but it falls short of the official, binding arbitration done in Toledo. A conference board should provide for this "review for discussion and advice" entry without assuming actual power for itself. In other words, it should establish a formal procedure for giving informal advice in a strike situation.

Type of membership. The Jackson board has seven members each of company president or directorship and union president rank. All are from manufacturing industries (except for the 15th member — the moderator). The Adrian board differed only in numbers: five from each.

The reasoning here was that industrial companies are most likely to be directly tied up with labor-management strife; other industries are on the periphery of labor relations and would make only a minimal contribution to the board. These two boards want only men of high rank, because they can actually change an industrial climate while their subordinates do not have such power.

The Sturgis board differs sharply in rank of members and type of affiliation. It includes a member from a retail, service or tourist group; one each from local government and a profession; and 10 from labor and management. No provision is made for rank.

This is done to bring an outside perspective into board discussions and decisions. Because community-wide issues are being talked about, the entire community should be represented. The Sturgis board also believes that because policy as such is not being made, top leaders do not necessarily have to be present to have their ideas expressed. An individual relatively removed from a central issue may be able to discuss it more objectively and may have more skill in group discussion than his superior. He may also have more latitude of discussion, since there is less chance that his comments will be construed as an official position of his company.

Official status of the board. The Jackson board is (and the

Adrian board was) a loose, informal organization held together only by the spirit of the membership.

Only the Sturgis board has a formal charter, articles of incorporation and statement of objectives which gives it a legal status. This status pushes the board into the limelight of publicity which Sturgis enjoys and Jackson and Adrian avoid.

On the one hand, shelter from public scrutiny is necessary for frank discussion. On the other, expansion and attraction of industry are aided by widespread recognition of the board's accomplishments. The Sturgis board resolves the dilemma best. It provides a regular flow of information to the public without binding any of its members or organizations to any specific position.

Voting. Because the Jackson board is and Adrian board was a purely-discussion kind of forum, they never could be in a position of having to vote on an issue.

But the Sturgis board is active as well as oral. If its mediatory function is ever called upon, it will have to issue advice; and if a consensus cannot be hammered out on what advice should be given, a vote will have to be taken. Similarly, in its publications the Sturgis board indicates whether consensus was reached on a point of discussion, and, if not, what management's feelings were and what labor's feelings were.

Any conference board, then, which will assume an active role in the community should devise a procedure for resolving internal disagreements when a common stand is necessary.

IV

How to Set Up and Run a Board

FORMATION

Proceeding to establish a local labor-management board requires a sensitive, well-considered strategy. Since the organizing may well take place in an atmosphere of suspicion and backbiting, consideration should be given to the seemingly mechanical details involved. The following guidelines are derived from the Jackson, Sturgis, and Adrian situations discussed in the previous chapters.

Who should form the board? Although the entire community may be aware that action is needed, there must be a starting point within it — one organization or representative of an organization to do the actual work. Necessity invariably dictates that this force not only be energetic, but neutral as well. Several examples: a local minister, lawyer, city official, representative of the State Employment Security Commission or the local industrial development corporation. These persons, above all, must have visibility in their city. They must be recognized for their interest in civic affairs and known to have the community's welfare in mind, not only labor or management or a segment thereof.

Although they may be able to function individually and not as members of an organization, their task will be easier if they act as envoys of the Chamber of Commerce, a mayor's committee, a local industrial development corporation (as in Jackson), or some other neutral group. They can then approach members of the community with the backing of an organization and make it known that they represent an established and respected group. Experience has shown that men may be reluctant to serve on a board only because no one had yet taken the initiative to start such a program. As seen above, once the first overtures had been made in Jackson, company representatives and union officials alike were quite willing to donate their time.

Advance information. Prospective board members and the community at large should be informed about the proposed venture. A common problem here is that the formulators frequently do not clearly know their course of action and, rather than appear foolish, avoid public discussion altogether. Yet if lack of communication retards labor-management cooperation, the extending of this attitude to the proposed remedy will hardly alleviate the sickness. A systematic procedure for disseminating information, therefore, should be initiated in the early planning stages and worked out with the local mass media.

Who should be approached personally? The natural tendency of the organizers is to go immediately to those whom they think will participate, excluding others who might be interested in the board and could lend a hand towards its success. But widespread support can be attained only if it is solicited on a widespread basis; the endorsement of a board from those who cannot serve or are personally unsuited for membership may help save the project from a rapid demise.

Representatives of unions and companies to be most directly affected and who are potential members should obviously be contacted well in advance of formation, but so should bankers, editors, builders, retailers and local government officials. They may be able to make valuable suggestions for the board and in so doing become involved themselves in its long-term operation. The founders should also seek the support of business and labor leaders who will not be charter board members so that they will encourage their colleagues to participate. This will tend to yield active support, not a passive acceptance.

Usually, a single exploratory meeting prior to the board's formation is not enough. It must be preceded by individual or small group contacts between founders and prospects. At this time, it is important to provide a broad statement of objectives supplemented by a brief summary of the need for a board. Although specific details need not (and perhaps could not) be spelled out, men cannot be expected to participate unless they are assured that their effort will be directed toward some realistic, worthwhile goal. Then need to know what the board will try to do and what it won't try to do; they have a right to know what they would be getting into. On a practical basis, this will help to dispel fears by management and labor that a new, apparently ominipotent body will be endangering their rights.

Who should serve on the board? Attributes most desirable are a willingness to serve, ability, sincerity and compatability. While it is good for each member to possess these virtues, the membership itself should be spread through the broadest possible base. The board should be composed of large and small business and a range of unions; no more than one man, either management or union, should represent any one company. A labor-management board is one place where monopoly, or even unbalance, of interest must not exist.

Members should have a definite term of office on a staggered basis, with a two-year period seeming most satisfactory. Having membership included from outside the immediate labor-management sphere, while not absolutely vital, may lend perspective to board discussions. The board need not necessarily be restricted to top-level personnel rank, but representatives should have some degree of power within their own organization to give the board influence and stature.

Choosing a moderator. Once members have been found, it becomes necessary to select a moderator with even greater care. He must be totally acceptable to the men with whom he will work, which means it is best for the members themselves to do the choosing as their first order of business.

The moderator will heavily influence the board's character, direction and impact. He will, after all, be guiding the discussions of a group that could decide whether a city will or will not thrive economically. He must, therefore, show his interest in the community welfare while at the same time observing strict neutrality and being attuned to the sensitivities of each member.

Possibilities for a moderator are the mayor, a clergyman, or other outsiders who are concerned with the future of their city. Jackson's moderators have been a priest, two ministers and a retired newspaper editor.

MAKING BOARD MEETINGS FRUITFUL

Frequency. Monthly meetings seem best. If held more often, they might degenerate into meaningless social hours. If held less often, they might become too general and noncontinuous. The intervals should be long enough for reflection and short enough for carryover.

Meetings of the Jackson, Sturgis and Adrian boards are traditionally held over dinner.

What to talk about. The topics should be whatever important, relevant things the members wish to discuss. They can range from broad national issues to specific local nuisances. Whatever the content, they should have a pragmatic orientation which relates the problem to local development and cooperation.

Some of the topics discussed by the Jackson board have already been presented in Chapter 2; a list of the ones considered by Sturgis appears in the appendix.

Closed or open meetings. If public attention did not inhibit discussion of business issues and problems, there would be little need for a board. But it does, and board meetings should thus be kept private. This should not, however, extend to the point of assuming an air of secrecy which would diminish public trust.

A good compromise is to invite various select outsiders from the public to meetings. Too many visitors would make the members feel as if they were under surveillance in a courtroom, but one or two guests will dispel secrecy and bring fresh views. Jackson's meetings have been attended by area planners, employment office experts, government officials and university professors who serve as speakers and observers. Members have found their visits quite helpful.

Record keeping. Board members generally prefer to have their comments remain off the record, so that spur-of-the-moment thoughts are not later misinterpreted as reasoned policy or official statements.

Yet a loose keeping of minutes, rather than a verbatim transcript, might prove of additional benefit while maintaining an encouragement to talk. They would not report exact individual comments, but would be limited to a record of attendance, names of guests, subjects of discussion, and any joint resolutions or statements of belief made and voted on by the board as a whole. This would ease the dissemination of information about the board, lend continuity and serve as a record.

Publicity. Although a board should operate in a degree of seclusion, it should make a determined effort to publicize its presence and its results. Not to do so defeats one major purpose of a conference board: to retain and attract industry.

Precautions should be taken, of course, to avoid misinterpretation by having members review and approve anything to be printed by the board. Most of the subjects it deals with affect the entire community; therefore, it assumes an obligation to keep that community well-informed about any conclusions it draws. The emphasis in publications should be on actions of the board, not individuals.

What powers should the board have? No inherent ones. As stated before, a board should mediate particular labor-management disputes upon request (and only upon request). Otherwise, a board which becomes entrapped in taking sides and punishing instead of building will soon find its communicative function dwindling away. Nor should its mediatory services detract from its primary purpose: improving the labor-management and economic climate.

The board should, however, establish a legal status for itself. The fact that Sturgis set up a formal charter, articles of incorporation and a statement of objectives has promoted its reputation of being a favorable area for plant location. It has a kind of official charter for doing so. The fact that Jackson's board has remained an informal, unincorporated one has helped its striving toward harmony but hampered the recognition of its achievements by industrial prospects.

Financing the board. It seems inappropriate to ask members to buy their own meals, as Adrian's board did, because the time and effort they put forth is not payment in itself. Nor should companies and unions be approached for financial support. It may not be fair to tax those who are not represented. On the other hand, donations from those who do volunteer their support might put the board on shaky and irregular financial ground. If, over a period of years, individual organizations cease to contribute, there would be little stimulus for others to step in and assume the burden.

By process of elimination, a local quasi-public group, such as an area development agency (as in Jackson), would seem to be the most feasible financial sponsor. Since the board attempts to serve the entire community, it is only fitting that the community share in assuming the cost of the service provided to it. Moreover, public agencies have existing means of soliciting funds, which would help to shape a general impression that the board will be a continuing activity with broad support. Any such organization that promoted the board in its formation stage might, of course, be a likely underwriter.

The costs will vary with each city, but it is reasonable to say that the amounts are relatively small. They are composed primarily of expenses for meeting place, meals, publications and outside speakers. While the latter two categories might be considered optional or marginal, there is little sense in skimping. Both have proved in practice to be a wise investment. Indeed, the costs should not be thought of as a burden, but as an investment in the future. And while it may be painful to spend, it may be even more painful not to. (As mentioned previously, the budget for the Jackson board in 1965 was only $40 per month for meals and incidentals.)

A WORD OF CAUTION

While the results of conference boards have ranged from

good to excellent, it should be pointed out that they were formed by individuals who did not operate impulsively. The founders will have to be willing to spend hours in molding policy for the proposed board, days in contacting prospective members and supporters, and years in actually working on labor-management problems.

Secondly, they must be able to distinguish between what is normal conflict among labor and management and what is abnormal and avoidable. They should not set out to supercede free-flowing business-worker relations, nor should they forget the necessity for labor arbitrators in particular labor-management disputes.

Finally, the founders should not delude themselves that an easy, obvious solution to their community's ills has been found. The boards discussed in this book are not a panacea or a utopia. But if properly organized and implemented, they can help to establish grass-roots industrial peace and area-wide economic development.

Appendix A

Following are excerpts from two of the bulletins published regularly by the Sturgis board. (The reader should recall that none of the other boards discussed has published materials for general distribution).

APRIL, 1962

The peak industrial employment in Sturgis was in 1958, at which time approximately 5,300 people were actively employed by Sturgis manufacturing companies.

At the present time, the industrial employment figure is about 4,200, a reduction of 1,100 jobs in four years.

At the time of the peak period in 1958 it was estimated that 47 per cent of the industrial employees working in Sturgis lived outside of the community — many as far as 50 miles.

During the recession period last spring, a study of the claims filed at the local Michigan Employment Office indicated that 38 per cent of the claiments had Sturgis addresses; 47 per cent had addresses outside of Sturgis; and 15 per cent had Indiana addresses.

Based on these percentage figures, a portion of the employment decline has been shared with other areas. Presently, the Michigan Employment Office lists approximately 1,000 unemployed in the St. Joseph County area.

Looking to the future, there will annually be approximately 150 to 250 local high school graduates and college graduates entering the labor market.

Sturgis likes its neighbors and wishes to help them in every way possible, and the board in no way intends that this bulletin suggests the replacement of employees not living in Sturgis. However, in view of the fact that Sturgis offers an adequate labor market from the ranks of its residents who pay taxes to provide city facilities and schools, it is the feeling of the board that in case of *new* hiring — all other things being equal — the applicant with the Sturgis address should be given preference.

The study by the board found many instances in the past where no apparent consideration has been given to the local applicant. Therefore, the attached resolution, drawn by the board and authorized by the Chamber Board of Directors, has been sent to all local employers.

NOVEMBER, 1963

The October 1963 meeting of the Sturgis Labor-Management Relations Board concluded three years of operations. At this particular meeting, the members reviewed the various items discussed and appraised the results of their efforts.

The broad range of discussion included such matters as:

Sturgis United Fund ... Labor climate in Sturgis ... Current employment situation ... What can be done to assist present industry and encourage its future growth in Sturgis ... Why does industry negotiating to leave keep the matter a secret until it is too late for local salvage operations ... Factors involved in some expansion and relocation to other states ... Legislative matters affecting industrial growth ... Moral obligations of employers to employees...Problems of giving technical assistance to foreign manufacturers ... Suggestion boxes ... Communications ... Who profits from profits ... What can we do to attract new industry — Business climate study ... Why does labor oppose the right-to-work law ... Community apathy.

Summarizing the activities, several definitions were placed upon *the functions of the board* by the following quotes of various members:

1) "A springboard approach to better understanding of the growth of the community through its industry and its employees."

2) "What an individual industry or union gets out of the board is immaterial. The main benefit to be derived is the overall improvement of understanding of our business community."

3) "Our exposure to the various methods of communication results in a better climate, not only for Sturgis, but also to the other communities which have investigated and copied our program."

4) "Fellowship that evolves permits the members to discuss problems on a more common level and has caused each to appreciate the fact that basically we are all individuals with the same hopes, desires and inspirations."

During the three years, no topic has been avoided and while the board is not a decision-making group, it does bring matters to light and illuminates the way for those who ultimately have to make the decisions.

While it is difficult to measure the tangible results, it is recognized that since the creation of this board, there has not been a strike or major labor unrest in Sturgis. Why? Perhaps it is because a chance comment made by one of the members might have remained with another member and thus had a definite bearing on a later decision that had to be made. Only in history, when it is written, can we look back and see whether there has been a total reduction of arbitration of severe strikes and labor problems and prove conclusively whether the board has been a contributing factor.

At this time the board makes its first major changes in membership, with the following individuals retiring and their counterparts taking replacement positions. . . .

As the board looked at the present and discussed the future it was agreed that the current industrial harmony would be felt by the entire community. As new prospects hear of our past problems, so they also must recognize that the problems are in the past and that a sound relationship now exists. Certainly, as this relationship and understanding continues to grow, all segments of the community will feel the results.

This board is not an arbitration group and cannot enter into any labor discussion unless specifically requested by those involved. It is hoped, however, that by discussing situations before they become problems the problems will thus be avoided.

DISSIMILARITIES BETWEEN THE BOARDS

	Jackson	Adrian	Sturgis
1. On rule of only one man from each company on the board	Concurs, reason is to obviate possibilities of unscheduled bargaining	Concurred, but reason was to get as many different companies as possible represented on the board	Concurs, same reason as Jackson
2. On length of membership on the board	Only provision is for dropping off the board by union officials who lose their office	No provision, wanted "lengthy" membership so members could "loosen up"	Two year terms of office
3. Entry into Labor Disputes	Non-entry as policy, although not strictly followed. Mediation is not uncommon	Same as Jackson	Possible to enter if formal request is made
4. Payment of bills	Paid by the Jackson Area Industrial Development Corporation	Members paid their own	Paid by the Chamber of Commerce
5. Publicity	Basically avoids publicity	Same as Jackson	Seeks publicity
6. Board Membership	Seven management, seven union, plus one moderator, minimum rank of president of company or local union, no two people from the same company	Same as Jackson except 5 and 5	One retail, service and tourist group member, one "professional" member, one "local government" member, one moderator and 5 each labor and management representatives, no two from the same company
7. Official Status of the Board	Undefined	Undefined	Official, formal recognition